Other *Easy Step by Step Guides*

Sales and Marketing Books
- Telemarketing, Cold Calling & Appointment Making
- Marketing
- Successful Selling
- Building a Positive Media Profile
- Writing Advertising Copy
- Writing Articles and Newsletters

Personal Development Books
- Stress and Time Management
- Communicating with more Confidence
- Giving Confident Presentations

Management Books
- Motivating Your Staff
- Recruiting the Right Staff
- Better Budgeting for your Business
- Managing Change
- Handling Confrontation
- Writing a Business Plan and Making it Work
- Negotiating for Success

Other books in the series
- Publishing and Promoting your Book
- Fundraising for your School

All the above guides are available from
bookshops and on line, and as eBooks

Rowmark Limited
E mail: enquiries@rowmark.co.uk
www.rowmark.co.uk

Books by Pauline Rowson

Crime Fiction – Marine Mysteries
- In Cold Daylight
- Tide of Death
- In for the Kill

Non-fiction
- Communicating With More Confidence
- Marketing
- Successful Selling
- Telemarketing, Cold Calling & Appointment Making
- Building a Positive Media Profile
- Fundraising for Your School
- Publishing and Promoting Your Book

Pauline Rowson

Pauline Rowson is author of several marketing and self-help books and for many years ran her own successful Marketing and PR Agency. Her first crime novel was published in 2006 after twenty years of writing fiction in which she never gave up on her dream of becoming a published and successful crime writer. Being positive and staying positive was essential when experiencing several knock-backs along the road to authorship. She is a frequent and popular speaker at conferences and workshops and has helped countless individuals to behave more assertively and take control of their lives.

Contents

Introduction

Changing work patterns, pressures of this fast-paced life, family problems, life cycle changes, and poor health can leave even the most positive of us feeling negative. So how do we cope when this happen? How do we resist the pressure to be all things to all men? How do we handle the guilt when we feel we are failing and inadequate? How can we learn to be more focused? And importantly how can we learn to get pleasure out of life when everything around us seems grim, or we have little or no time to appreciate it?

Read on. This book is a practical, self-help guide for anyone who wants to become more positive and stay positive – even when the going gets tough!

What you will learn

○ how to find contentment with yourself

○ how to increase your self confidence

○ how to realize your full potential

○ how to stop being frustrated with life and start living it

○ how to benefit from being positive and staying positive even when things get difficult

○ how to handle difficult people and situations and keep calm.

How to use this guide

This guide is written in as clear a style as possible to aid you. I recommend that you read it through from beginning to end and then dip into it to refresh your memory. The boxes in each chapter contain tips to help you, and at the end of each chapter there is a useful at-a-glance summary of the points covered.

Chapter 1

Why should we be positive?

Given the pressures in life, and the pace of change today, it is not always easy to maintain a positive attitude especially when you are working too hard, or when things don't seem to be going right in your personal life. Perhaps you are trying to cram too much into your life, or you are trying to please too many people at the expense of your own feelings and wants. Whatever your circumstances and the situation when you are feeling negative it is difficult to make rational decisions and see the options that are available.

If you do not know the techniques to help you through these trying times, or you do not have the confidence to speak out, or seek advice when needed, then you will feel that your life is out of control. Subsequently a sense of hopelessness can swamp you. This can lead to more dangerous feelings such as depression. It is important, therefore, to understand what makes you feel negative, and to do something about it, no matter how small.

> **Small steps lead to bigger ones, which in turn can lead to giant steps on the road to a more fulfilling and positive life.**

But how do you do this? The first step on the road to becoming positive is to *want* to. The second is to train yourself to *think* positively even when the going gets tough.

But what if I am a natural pessimist?

Indeed some people, whether through upbringing or personality (or both), may have a somewhat pessimistic outlook on life. Do you find yourself constantly moaning, or feeling bitter and resentful? Do you view the glass as half empty rather than half full? If so, then take heart from the fact that you are reading this book, and that you *want* to change that outlook. If on the other hand you are quite happy to be miserable then you might as well stop reading now, and either give this book to someone else, or throw it away.

Great! You've decided to read on to see how you can find contentment with yourself, how you can increase your self confidence, how you can stop being frustrated with life, and how you can benefit from being positive and staying positive.

**Having a positive outlook can
seriously benefit your health.**

The benefits of being positive

There are many benefits of being positive. Here are
some:

○   there is an increased chance of your needs being
met

○   you will have greater confidence in yourself

○   you will have greater confidence in others

○   you will be able to take more initiatives

○   you will have greater self control and higher self
worth

○   there will be no see-sawing of emotions

○   more options will open up for you

All this leads to

⬇

A reduction in stress

⬇

Better personal health

⬇

Increased energy and efficiency

In addition, positive people attract *more* positive people and, as a result, are more successful in their professional and personal lives.

And if you're still not convinced here are some further reasons for being and staying positive:

- you will suffer less negative stress
- gain greater co-operation from others
- lead a more contented and fulfilling life.

What further reasons could you want?

What makes you feel negative?

To make a start on this journey to becoming a more positive and self-confident person let's first understand what makes us feel negative.

Negative emotions are:

O   Anger
O   Frustration
O   Being upset

Exercise
Without looking at the list on page 17 try this exercise. Write down all the things that make you feel negative i.e. angry, upset and frustrated. This can include things that happen in the workplace, at home or any other aspect of your life.

When you have made your list you might like to ask a friend to do the same exercise and then compare lists.

You may find similarities, but you may also find that what makes your friend feel negative doesn't necessarily have the same effect on you. This is because we all react to stressful occurrences in different ways; indeed what stresses one person may not stress another.

> **Knowing what makes you feel negative is a step towards becoming more positive.**

Here are some things that make people feel negative, you may have them on your list:

○ the weather
○ being stuck in a traffic jam
○ not being appreciated either at home or at work
○ too much work and not enough time to do it
○ being bored
○ being constantly criticized
○ bereavement
○ family or relationship breakdown
○ being ill
○ a difficult or awkward person
○ seemingly endless pointless rules and regulations
○ never enough time
○ too much to do
○ being let down
○ having too high expectations of others and myself
○ lack of information and poor communication

In the following chapters we are going to look at how to handle negativity in others and ourselves, how to boost our self-confidence and our self-esteem and how to take control of our lives.

What to aim for

A mature personality is what we are aiming for. This can be defined as being the following:

O   The ability to identify with other people's concerns as well as with our own; to offer sympathy and empathy

O   A warm unselfish relationship with others

O   The absence of suspicion and resentment

O   Emotional security

O   Living in the present and the future – not the past, learning to let go

O   Being realistic about yourself

O   Having a realistic view of the world

O   The ability to exercise sound judgment and take
    necessary decisions

O   Not wasting time and energy fighting conditions
    you cannot change

O   Co-operation with life instead of trying to destroy
    it or run away from it

O   The ability to take the initiative and responsibility
    for your own actions

O   Refusing to pity yourself

O   Not expecting too much of yourself

O   Some consistent view of the meaning of life,
    whether it be religious or humanistic, that helps
    you set values and determine life goals

In summary

O   Having a positive outlook can seriously benefit your health

O   *Wanting* to be more positive is the first step towards becoming more positive

O   You need to understand what makes you feel negative

O   A mature personality is what you are aiming for.

Chapter 2

How to cope with negative feelings

Understanding what is controllable and uncontrollable?

I would like you to look at the list you have made on what causes you to feel negative. Now identify all the things on your list that you feel are beyond your control.

On first glance you may feel that everything on your list is uncontrollable. The weather, for example, is beyond our control, being caught in a traffic jam is beyond our control, falling ill could be beyond our control, bereavement is beyond our control, being unappreciated at work is beyond our control and so on. Even if we say everything on our list is uncontrollable there is one factor in all of this that is within our control and that is **our reaction to the event, circumstance or the person.**

Our inner voice

The way we react to an event, person or circumstance is determined by what we are thinking, by the dialogue that is being conducted inside our head. I like to call this our **inner voice.** This inner voice could be a negative one. If so, it could lead us to react to events and people in a negative way by getting angry or becoming upset.

We need to hear this negative inner voice, recognize it for what it is, and change it to a positive inner voice. This will mean that we will then react to people and events in a much more positive way.

There are some life-changing events such as the loss of a loved one, a relationship breakdown, and illness that take tremendous courage to deal with, and you may need more in-depth help to get you through these traumatic experiences than this book can provide, but *recognizing* that you need practical or spiritual help is a positive step forward.

Now, looking at the other things on your list in comparison to the three I have just mentioned above don't they seem trivial? Getting things into their proper perspective is one technique to help you to become

more positive and stay positive. I look at this in more detail in chapter four, which examines values and goal setting.

So, to get back to our list of negative things, let's see how we can change the way we react to these negative elements.

Take the weather.

In Britain the weather is always a topic of conversation. It is not unknown to have four seasons in one day and certainly in one week. Continuous rain and grey skies, high winds and the cold can make us all feel low. We wake up in the morning, pull up the blinds and groan at yet another grey, miserable day. The conversation inside our heads can go something like this:

> 'It's raining again. I'm fed up with this weather – it really gets me down. I know it's going to be a horrible day today. I wish I were in the sunshine somewhere and not stuck here doing this.'

Can you hear the negativity in this dialogue? If this is going through your mind then you are conditioning your brain to feel depressed. As a result your body language will go into a downward spiral, which in turn

sends negative messages back to your brain because, believe it or not, the brain and body are connected! So the brain goes into an even greater downward spiral. As a result you snap at the kids, you grumble at your partner, you drive to work too fast and get cross with someone who cuts you up; the traffic seems worse than usual and the radio has nothing but bad news on it, or the train arrives late and is too crowded. By the time you get to work (if you have a job) you are feeling thoroughly disgruntled. What kind of day are you going to have? You've guessed it – a very bad day.

So let's rewind.

You pull up the blinds, and you look at the weather and say, 'It's raining again. Never mind. If we didn't have the rain we wouldn't appreciate the sunshine. I can still have a good day today, and I am going to have a good day.'

I can't guarantee that the trains will then arrive on time, or that the motorways will be traffic and accident free, or that your children won't be fighting, but it will start the day for you in a positive frame of mind rather than a negative one and that positivity, if maintained, will rub off on other people and create yet more positivity.

You need to train your brain to think in this way, and you can by recognizing the negative inner dialogues and converting them to positive ones. Positive dialogues inside your head will send positive messages to your body, your shoulders will go back and your body language will be positive, which in turn sends positive signals back to the brain. A win-win situation. I will cover more on the inner voice in chapters four and ten.

Reframing

There is a wonderful expression in marketing and indeed political circles – it is called reframing. For example, the general is not retreating he is simply advancing in a different direction!

There is always another way of looking at things and, if you train your brain properly, you will see this. I can't recall who said 'there is no such thing as bad weather only bad clothing,' but whoever did was looking at the weather from a different angle – that's reframing.

The window of opportunity

So you've started your day well with a positive inner voice, and then you get stuck in a traffic jam. Now you

have, what I call, a small window of opportunity in which to choose how to react. You can get stressed out and go into negative mode, or you can accept the inevitable delay and go into positive mode. Instead of reacting angrily, and ranting and raving at the hold up, your positive inner dialogue could go something like this:

> 'I'm stuck in this traffic jam; there's nothing I can do about it. Getting angry won't make the traffic move any faster. I can call the office/home/ my friend to let them know I am going to be late. I can put some music on the radio/tape/CD and be patient.'

Let others around you get stressed and have high blood pressure – it won't make the traffic move any faster. One way to look at this is whilst you are stuck in traffic someone could be fighting for his or her life ahead of you. Isn't it selfish that all we can think about is how it has inconvenienced us? You're alive and breathing – better late than never as the old saying goes.

There are other occasions when you need to recognize this window and switch on your spilt second positive inner dialogue. Perhaps someone is being rude to you, or the person you dread the most is heading towards

you, or a piece of equipment fails at the crucial moment. You have the opportunity to choose how to react. You need to train yourself to see that split second and trigger your positive response: 'I can keep calm,' will work for many people or 'I can handle this,' is another positive message. Saying this mentally, or aloud, will send a positive message to your brain, your brain will in turn prime your body to respond in this way. Once this split second dialogue has kicked in you can then take a bit more time to examine your feelings, and change the negative dialogue going through your brain to a positive one.

Comfort Zone

But what if your lifestyle means you are continually getting stressed. Is the pressure of commuting becoming too much to cope with? Are you trying to cram too much into your life? Are you stuck in a job you hate, or in a relationship that is going nowhere?

Changing your job, partner or lifestyle is not easy, and indeed you may be thinking it's impossible. 'Impossible' like the word 'never' is a BIG word – an exaggerated word. Never is a long time. And impossible? Is it really impossible? If you are feeling particularly negative whilst reading this book you might be saying to yourself

I **CAN'T** change things. I'm trapped. This is a negative dialogue? You need to change this to a positive one. You need to:

- 𝄞 Hear it
- ᘒ Recognize it
- ✋ Challenge it
- ☺ Change it

As I have already said being positive means you are able to see options. There are always options. Don't allow yourself to get stuck on the obstacles.

> **The person who has the most options has the less negative stress.**

Moving out of your comfort zone is not easy. It takes courage and creativity. But you CAN do it. Often it is the fear of failure that prevents us from taking that first step into the unknown and hence we put it off. We make excuses. I know that it is not always easy to see the solutions immediately, particularly if you are stressed, and it may take you time to change your lifestyle, but thinking about it, and then forming an action plan to change it will help you become less

stressed and get you moving in a positive direction.

Ask yourself some questions: do you need to travel as much as you do? Can you find a different job closer to home? Can you cut down your hours, or job share? Do you need to reorganise your finances? Do you really need that big house? Are you trying to live beyond your means or keep up with the Jones's? Are you trying to fit too much into your life? Does something have to go? Can you get a better balance? Or do you like being indispensable because it boosts your self worth? Is the relationship not working? Why? Do you need to see a counsellor or be more open with your partner? Do you need help in moving out of a difficult or violent relationship? Examine your answers to these questions, or the ones that are really bothering you? How honest have you been?

A good way to work through a problem is to try and formulate it. Identify the real nature of the problem by running through all the various scenarios that are causing it. Try looking at it from a number of angles.

For example:

> 'I am unhappy because I am not getting the recognition I deserve at work. This is because the boss doesn't like me.'

OR

> 'I am unhappy because I don't like the boss.'

OR

> 'I am unhappy at work and not getting promotion because I don't have the right qualifications.'

OR

> 'I am unhappy at work because my problems at home have been distracting me of late.'

When you stop to think about the problem, and to consider the greater range of explanations for it, you will have a wider and less predictable range of options open out for you.

Do you know what you really want? I examine goals in chapter four, which could help you with this.

Here is what happened to me some years ago. I had a very good job as head of Marketing and PR for an international firm of chartered accountants. The salary package was generous and each year I had a new company car. To some people I had it made, and yet

increasingly I was unhappy and couldn't define why. One day I was driving along the motorway to work when it suddenly struck me that I'd rather be cleaning toilets than doing the job. I was bored. Yes, the revelation was that drastic. I knew then I had to do something about it. At the time Britain was in the middle of a recession and it wasn't easy to change jobs, besides getting a similar job meant commuting and I knew I didn't want to spend my life sitting on a train or on a motorway. I had always had an ambition to run my own business, and decided that if I was going to do it now was the time. It took me another year before I could hand in my resignation. During that year I scrimped and saved, the only new clothes I bought were from charity shops, until I had some money behind me, which would help me over the first few difficult months until I could get some clients. When I handed in my resignation I was asked if I would stay on as a consultant for six months, something I hadn't planned for but which suited me very well, and what's more I was paid more as a consultant on a one day a week basis than as an employee. I never looked backed.

The fear of failure could have prevented me from taking that first step and I'd still be trapped in a job I didn't find fulfilling.

Sometimes we are forced out of our comfort zone by circumstances, a redundancy or a marital break up. Sometimes we need others to give us the push, but why wait for that? Does it really matter if you fail or shall we say fail to achieve what you set out in the first place? Think what you have gained along the way. No experience is ever wasted. You *will gain* something from it. By having a positive outlook you can learn from your experiences, and move onwards.

> **You can sit at home wishing until the cows come home but unless you ACT nothing will change.**

One final word on this, instead of asking yourself what you want to achieve ask yourself what you *want?* Is it to make other people happy? To be more creative? To be happier? Try writing it down, or come back to this after we have looked at values in chapter four.

Now let's look at some of the other negative elements on our list from chapter one:

○   not being appreciated either at home or at work
○   being constantly criticized

You may feel that these are out of your control because how can you change the person who is constantly criticizing you? How can you be more appreciated?

Firstly I want to stress that you cannot change another person so forget that idea for a start. Many people waste a great deal of time and energy trying to change others and become very disappointed and frustrated because they fail to do so, and are constantly let down.

You are the only person that can change you. Take responsibility for yourself. Take charge of yourself.

You can only change yourself.

By changing your attitude, outlook, and behaviour you will change the reaction you get from others. So instead of complaining that Bill is always on your back moaning at you, or that your boss doesn't appreciate you, or that you've got too much work to do, recognize the negative dialogue in your head: you are moaning or grumbling, you are being pessimistic and you are not in control of your own life and emotions.

𝄢   Hear the negative voice

ℰ   Recognize it

✋   Challenge it

☺   Change it

And here I will add three further things:

Know yourself

Appreciate yourself

Speak out for yourself

We will see how to do this in the following chapters.

In summary

○   Our inner voice is within our control. We can choose how we react to a situation, event or person

○   Understand that not everything is controllable in life but that your mental reaction and your inner voice is controllable

○   Recognize the window of opportunity you have and choose how you wish to react

O No experience is ever wasted. You can always learn from things even if they seem a disaster at the time

O You can choose to get stressed out and go into negative mode or you can choose to go into positive mode

O Positive people have more options

O Take responsibility for yourself. Take charge of yourself

O You can only change yourself

O By changing your attitude, outlook, behaviour you will change the reaction you get from others.

O Recognize the negative dialogue in your head:

   𝄞 Hear it
   ᧒ Recognize it
   ✋ Challenge it
   ☺ Change it

O Know yourself, appreciate yourself, speak out for yourself

Chapter 3

Understanding stress

Returning to your list of negative things did you have written down too much to do, not enough time? Life is about getting a balance. You can't do everything. Time is finite there are only so many minutes in an hour, hours in day and days in a year. None of us know how much time is allotted to us on this earth. We do not have forever and it is what we do with our time while here that counts. You need to apportion that time and importantly allow time for yourself as well as for others. You cannot do everything yourself and if you try, or believe you can, then it could be a short ticket to the cemetery.

There are many pressures on us to do lots of things and to be all things to all men; good wives, mothers, career women, successful men, high flyers. Many people at some time (or even many times throughout their lives) feel that they cannot cope with their jobs, their families, their responsibilities, or their lives. Recognizing this and the fact that you are not alone helps. Doing something about it will change those feelings and help you take control.

Realistic expectations

Unrealistic expectations may have been something else that you had on your list of what makes you feel negative. It may not only be expectations of yourself, but also the expectations you have of others. If your expectations are too high, and can't be met, you will face disappointment and frustration.

Our expectations are much higher than those of our parents and grandparents. Whilst aiming high is to be encouraged it can also produce negative feelings because some of those expectations, especially material and lifestyle ones, are unrealistic; they are beyond our means to achieve. This makes us resentful and discontented. For example if we don't have the shiny new car or the holiday abroad then we can be made to feel guilty and inadequate.

Taking stock of what you have, and examining your values, can help you to readjust your expectations to the levels that you are happy with. If you are continually comparing what you have with others and find yourself lacking you will become bitter and resentful and cause yourself additional negative stress. A return to valuing the simple things in life can prove to be invigorating and liberating.

Finding out what is really important to you can sometimes come after experiencing a shock such as bereavement. Only then do we realize how trivial some of the things we have been worrying about and striving for really are.

Some disasters can also cause us to re evaluate our lives, like a flood or fire. And natural events can also help us to put our lives and expectations into perspective. I remember watching the eclipse. The traffic in the town where I was at the time fell silent and everyone stopped what they were doing to gaze up at the sky. People came out of offices, shops and factories. As I gazed up through special spectacles at the eclipse I wondered what would happen if the sun never came out again. I realized that we are all at the mercy of nature and that if the sun didn't emerge having the shiny new car wouldn't matter one jot!

The right amount of stress

But we all need some stress. The right amount of stress is good for us; it can lead to increased motivation and satisfaction. Too little stress and we'd be bored or dead! However, what stresses one person will not necessarily stress another so you need to know how much stress you can take before it becomes unhealthy. You also need to know the things that cause you stress and so avoid them, or find ways of dealing with them.

Your stress levels can change with your age. What you found exhilarating at twenty could knock you flat at forty. The lifestyle you find comfortable in your thirties, with its hard work, gruelling timetable balancing home and kids could be very stressful when you hit your forties. Our bodies and minds change as we go through our lifecycle and we need to recognize this and not be surprised by it.

Research has shown that women experiencing the double shift of work and home have greater stressors than men. I have met many women in their early forties and mid to late fifties who are quite literally worn out. They are suffering high degrees of stress from a lifetime of balancing both worlds, trying to resolve the mental and physical conflict this has brought.

Another high stress age is that of retirement. The busy working man or woman can have status, purpose, responsibility one day and nothing the next. We all need a framework for our lives and for many of us work provides it. When that framework goes we are left floundering. We feel useless. We feel that we don't belong anywhere and this can lead to high stress levels and illness. We need to prepare for retirement, and create a new framework for ourselves.

This kind of stress is sometimes also experienced by young people leaving school particularly those 'difficult' children who frequently play truant and often have an unhappy home life. They can't wait to leave the school they hate, but when they do teachers often find them coming back, or hanging about outside the gates because the school was the only stable framework they had in their lives. Once it is gone they don't know how to create a new one.

How do you recognize high levels of stress?

High levels of stress are associated with higher rates of nervousness, feelings of tenseness, restlessness, an inability to relax and a sense of being pressed for time.

If not acted upon the results can be:

O   Higher blood pressure, which can lead to strokes and heart attack

O   More infections

O   Stomach ulcers

O   Depression and mental ill health

O   Increased smoking or drinking of alcohol and caffeine

Do you recognize any of these? Try the questionnaire on the next page to see if you are suffering from negative stress.

Questionnaire

During the last month have you continually felt any of the things listed below?

Keyed up and on edge	Yes☐	No☐
Irritable	Yes☐	No☐
Mood swings	Yes☐	No☐
Tearful	Yes☐	No☐
Difficulty in relaxing and sleeping	Yes☐	No☐
Headaches	Yes☐	No☐
Low energy	Yes☐	No☐
A tendency to feel worse in the mornings even after a good night's sleep	Yes☐	No☐

If you have answered yes to over four of these questions then heed the danger signs now and do something about it. If you don't, you could fall ill.

I mentioned before that different people have different levels of stress. If you are what is known as a Type A personality then your stress threshold may be high. Type A personalities are people who are strivers and high achievers. Although generally speaking they can take a greater amount of pressure than others they are also more prone to stress. This is because they don't know when to ease the foot off the gas and as a

consequent ignore the danger signs. This in turn can lead to burn out and illness.

Type A's often thrive on stress, probably because their bodies manufacture more than the normal amount of noradrenalin, the stress hormone which is associated with confidence and elation. This can become addictive because it creates a 'high.' They seek out more stressful situations and become 'hooked' on it. But at some stage this will become counterproductive, the body cannot keep this high level going indefinitely. We have all experienced moments of elation and then afterwards wondered why we felt flat and sometimes rather depressed. If a Type A becomes addicted to stress he/she will be in danger of collapse at some time, which could be fatal.

Overachievers are also at risk from stress related illnesses. These are people who always seem to cope, who refuse to give in to illness and fatigue and take on demands of others often at their own expense. They can deny the possible dangers of stress until their health suffers.

You may be neither of the above but a fairly steady, dependable sort of person, normally quite content, you like routine and the status quo. However the world is

changing fast and change may be forced upon you at work or in your personal life. This can cause you a considerable amount of stress, which if not recognized and acted upon, could lead to poor health.

Are you are a striver?

Here is a quick and simple test.

Do you like to win at everything?	Yes☐	No☐
Are you a team player?	Yes☐	No☐
Do you like to do several things at the same time?	Yes☐	No☐
Do you have a tendency to finish people's sentences for them?	Yes☐	No☐
Are you impatient when thwarted?	Yes☐	No☐
Do you ever use the phrase 'I don't tolerate fools very easily'?	Yes☐	No☐
Are you always in a rush, talking quickly eating food quickly?	Yes☐	No☐

If you have scored all yes's, or a high proportion of yes's then you are a striver. You need to recognize this and find ways to unwind and develop a less driven approach, difficult I know, but essential to your well-being.

Coping with stress

Knowing what makes you feel negative and what causes you stress will help you to handle it. As will the techniques detailed in this book. Here are some further techniques to help you cope with stress.

If you are feeling under pressure and experiencing stress try talking about it to someone.
This can be difficult, particularly for men, who do not naturally confide what they perceive to be their weaknesses to others, but talking *does* help.

Take time to think about yourself and how you are feeling.
By being more aware of yourself and your feelings you are more likely to pick up on stress. Hopefully this book will help you to do this.

Take part in a sport or arts activity.
Physical and/or creative activity is a terrific outlet for stress.

Eat a healthy, well-balanced diet.

Be sensible about how much alcohol you drink.

Get help to give up smoking.

Get enough sleep and rest to recharge your energy levels.

Work no more than ten hours daily.

Have at least one and a half days free each week from normal work routine.

Learn to accept what you cannot change.

Know when you are tired and do something about it.
Don't push yourself too hard. If you are sick then don't try to carry on as if you are not.

Manage your time better.
Delegate if you can, say 'no' sometimes. (see chapter nine).

Agree with someone.
Life should not be a constant battleground.

If emotional and/or sexual relationships are distressing you seek advice.

If you are unhappy at work, take stock and look at choices.

If you have done something stressful, don't go onto another stressful activity, give yourself a break.

Create stress free corridors: do something different, go home a different way, treat yourself.

And if you are the sort of person who is always in a rush then here are some tips for you:

○   Try to restrain yourself from being the centre of attention

○   Force yourself to listen to others

○   Stop trying to finish their sentences for them

○   Ask yourself:
  ❑   Do I really have anything important to say?
  ❑   Does anyone really want to hear it?
  ❑   Is this the right time to say it?

○   Must you do it right now or do you have enough time to think about the best way to accomplish it?

In summary

○　Negativity can lead to harmful stress which if not corrected will in turn lead to poor health

○　Life is about getting a balance. You can't do everything

○　Learn to trust and respect yourself and others

○　The right amount of stress is good for us – it can lead to increased motivation and satisfaction. Too little stress and you'd be bored or dead!

○　If you are suffering from negative stress talk to someone

○　Take part in a sport or arts activity

○　Take time to think about yourself and how you are feeling

○　Be more aware of yourself and your feelings

○　Eat a healthy, well-balanced diet

○　Be sensible about how much alcohol you drink

○　Get help to give up smoking.

Chapter 4

Know yourself

The better you know yourself the easier it is for you to recognize what triggers your negative emotions and adopt the correct techniques to cope with them.

Many of us though do not take the time to get know ourselves because we have been conditioned that to think about ourselves is self indulgent, selfish and arrogant. **It is not**.

Self-confidence is not the same as over confidence. Being self-confident recognizes that you know your faults as well as your strengths. Being over confident means that you do not recognize your faults or, certainly if you do, you do not acknowledge them to yourself or to others. Humility is fine and is to be applauded so long as it is accompanied by self-knowledge and self-awareness, which lead to self-confidence. If humility is accompanied by low self-esteem and feelings of worthlessness then it is not fine.

Get to know yourself Questionnaire

Try answering some of these questions

1. What am I good at?

2. What am I bad at?

3. What do I most like doing?

4. What do I most dislike doing?

5. What types and levels of people can I mix freely with?

6. What type of role do I tend to take?

- ❑ Lead
- ❑ Drive
- ❑ Arbitrate

7. How do other people describe me?

8. What words describe me in general terms?

9. What attainments am I most proud of?

10. Where do I see myself in five years time?

11. What would I like to become?

Some of the questions are difficult to answer and you may have to think about them for some time. If you are feeling particularly low, or have poor self-esteem, you may have struggled to answer the question: 'What am I good at?' and may have written reams under the question: 'What am I bad at?' Everyone is good at something you just need to find and refine it. If you have a close friend or colleague, whose opinions you value and trust, then enlist their help in doing this exercise.

'What do I want to become?' Now that is a difficult question, or is it? Perhaps another way of looking at this would be to ask the question, 'How do I want to be remembered when I am are gone?'

Defining what we want in life is not always easy because we don't always know. We have to strip away preconceptions before we can see the options. We can begin to do this by looking at our values and setting goals.

Your values

Knowing what you value in life and keeping these constantly in mind will not only help you to find direction but will also help you deal with difficult

situations and difficult people. Often when we are under stress and feeling negative things get out of proportion. You need to get a sense of perspective back in your life. You need to know what you value.

Exercise
Take a piece of paper and list on it all the things that you value in your life, everything that is significant in it, for example: your partner, your children, your health.

Think long and hard about them. Can you prioritize them? It isn't always easy.

I often do this exercise with my students as it helps me to revaluate where I am going with my life. It was quite a shock to me a short while ago to realize that my life was out of kilter.

For years I had been working hard, striving to get to the top and eventually running my own business and yet I realized that work had taken over my life. I had nothing outside of work except my relationship with my long-suffering and very patient husband and I was even putting that at risk! My life consisted of getting up, working nearly twelve hours a day, coming home, glass or two of wine, eating, crashing out and sleeping.

I found myself constantly thinking of work and waking up with the three o'clock horrors, that's when you lie there worrying about everything and anything unable to get back to sleep.

The next morning I would feel tired and the whole cycle would begin again. I was finding that I was getting through the days by going from one appointment to another wishing my life away – crazy!

I am sure many of you reading this book will be able to identify with this. I know from the number of people I meet on my courses there are many who feel that their life is out of control. One lady said to me that all she wanted to do was to cook a nice meal for her family and serve it up instead of taking food from the freezer to the microwave and plonking it on the table. She didn't have time to do anything else. She **wanted time**. And yet she had been offered promotion, which meant more hours spent working. In the end, after examining her values, and what she wanted out of life, she refused the promotion, cut down her hours, and although she wasn't richer in monetary terms she was richer in time.

I needed to get the balance back into my life. I did this by first looking at my values.

My values before this experience read something like this:

Successful
Career
Achievements
Respected
Status
Liked
Husband
Health

Now revisiting them they read:

Health
Husband
Family
Creativity
Fulfillment
Social

Prioritizing them is difficult as joint top would be health and husband.

Exercise

Now take another piece of paper and divide it down the middle and then into squares or boxes. The number of squares you need will depend on how many things you listed in your values exercise. Put a value heading in each box.

For Example

Partner/Husband	Children
Health	Social life
Hobbies	Religion/Faith

Goals

In order to give you focus you need to think about your goals for each of your values. Goals might be:

○   to spend more time with my partner
○   to help my children more with their schoolwork
○   to get fitter
○   to visit and help my parents more
○   to spend more time developing my hobby
○   to see my friends more often and make time for them

Put your goals under the headings in each box.

Once the goals have been added you then need to think about how you are going to achieve them. Some goals may take you longer to achieve than others. And some may seem quite daunting when you first look at them. For example under health you might wish to give up smoking and perhaps you are saying to yourself 'I shall never be able to do that. I tried once and failed.' Can you hear the negative dialogue here? Did you have a negative voice on any of your goals? If you did then remember how to tackle it:

- Hear it
- Recognize it
- Challenge it
- Change it

In the previous example I used the word 'never.' Never is a long time. It is an exaggerated word. Every time you hear that word challenge it.

There is an old maxim, 'Adults fail because they expect to fail.' If you think you will fail then you most invariably will. So let's change that negative voice.

Rewind:
'I know it's going to be tough giving up smoking (or chocolate/alcohol/changing my job) but I **can** do it. I can take it step by step. I can seek help and I can do it.'

Make sure your goals are positive goals; about things you *want* to do with your life not things you wish to get rid of, for example to get fit is a positive goal rather than I want to stop feeling such a slob!

Goals will also need to be:

- ❑ measurable
- ❑ achievable
- ❑ realistic
- ❑ timed

You will need to put in a measurement otherwise how will you know when you are fit? What do you define as being fit? When would you like to achieve this fitness level by? Is this achievable? The worst thing you can do is to set yourself unrealistic goals because if you don't meet them you will be disappointed. You may be better able to flesh out your goals, and the timetable for achieving them, when you have put in place the steps required to reach that goal.

Example Goal

To get fit so that I can run two miles easily (or climb a hill without stopping half way up) by (and put a date).

Steps

Now you need to look at your goals and underneath each put in the steps you can take to reach your goal.

For example:

Partner
Goal: To spend more time with my partner/ husband/wife.
Step: Starting from Monday I will come home early from work at least once a week and enjoy a meal with my partner.

Yes, it needs to be that basic. If you are working long hours then making this commitment to come home early, or leaving work at your allotted time one day a week, will be a big step for you. Set the goal, take the first step and stick to it no matter what. It will be tough but you **CAN** do it.

Fitness/Health
Goal: To get fit so that I can run two miles easily (or climb a hill without stopping half way up) by (and put a date).
Steps: To walk at least twenty minutes three days a week. **Or:** To cycle three miles once a week.

And what if your goal is to give up smoking, drinking alcohol, eating chocolate or similar?

Finding out why you drink, smoke, eat too much, or why you feel you can't change your lifestyle is important, and the reasons may be embedded deep inside you. You may find you need help taking the first step on this road.

When do you reach for the wine bottle, or the cigarette? Why do you feel the need for it? What are your feelings? If you can identify them you may be able to identify what makes you smoke, eat or drink too much. What can you do instead of abusing your health? Can you go for a walk, take up a hobby, read a book, pick up the telephone and talk to a friend or relative? Find something that can help you take your mind off the matter.

Positive thinking

When setting your goals, and trying to attain them, it is important to have the right dialogue in your head. If you tell yourself you are fat then you will be thinking fat and you will stay that way. If you tell yourself that only *you* have control over what *you* put in your mouth then you are taking control of your mind and not

conditioning it to be negative. You will find it much easier to give up sweets, chocolates and cakes etc.

If you need to improve your diet then don't feel you have to change all your eating habits at once. Take **steps** to change it.

You can take responsibility for your own life. *You* can take control of it – no one else can. There isn't a magic pill that will change you or your circumstances; only *you* can make it happen.

How to wake up in the morning feeling positive

Before you go to sleep at night instead of lying there worrying about all the things that you need to do the next day, why not focus your mind on something that you are looking forward to. It doesn't matter what it is, or how trivial, just as long as it something that excites you. If you can't think of anything then take some time to reflect on your life, work on your values and goals. If your life is such that you have nothing to look forward to each day then you need to take some action. Perhaps you need to move out of your comfort zone by tackling that problem at work, or personal relationship? Perhaps it doesn't have to be quite so drastic; discovering a

hobby, taking greater pleasure in what you do at work, giving something back to the community in which you live could all give you a positive fix.

If all you are looking forward to is your holiday in six months time, then what is happening to your life in the intervening period? Aren't you wishing it away?

Before you fall asleep focus on the positive aspects of your life. Re read your list of values to remind yourself what you have got going for you.

If you wake up in the middle of the night worrying then find techniques to deal with this. The more you worry about getting back to sleep the less likely you are. If you are saying to yourself, 'I *can't* sleep,' or 'I'll *never* get back to sleep,' then you won't. You are priming your brain *not* to sleep. Instead, try re framing this. 'I may not be asleep, but I am still resting and relaxing.'

Sometimes it helps to jot down what is worrying you, having done this you can then shelve the problem and return to sleep. So keeping a notepad and pen beside your bed might help. Getting up for a short while can help, or reading a chapter of a book. Don't be tempted to drink a cup of coffee, as that will only keep you awake.

Before retiring establish a routine that will help you sleep: take a shower or hot bath, drink a cup of hot milk, don't drink too much alcohol or have a heavy meal too soon before retiring, go for a walk, read a book. Then focus on all the positive things you have going for you in your life, and at least one thing you are looking forward to the next day.

In summary

○ The better you know yourself the more able you are to cope with negative stresses

○ Self-confidence is not the same as over confidence

○ Being self-confident recognizes that you know your faults as well as your strengths. Being over confident means that you do not recognize your faults or, you do not acknowledge them

○ Knowing what you value in life, and keeping these constantly in mind, will help you deal with difficult situations and people by getting things into perspective

O   Make sure your goals are positive goals; about things you want to do with your life not things you wish to get rid of

O   Goals also need to be:

  ❏   measurable
  ❏   achievable
  ❏   realistic
  ❏   timed

O   When setting your goals it is important to have a positive inner voice

O   You have to take responsibility for your own life. You can take control of it – no one else can.

Chapter 5

Assertiveness

Assertiveness is a characteristic of behaviour not of a person. We are not born assertive: it is something that we need to learn. Why? Because it leads to better health.

What is an assertive person?

An assertive person is someone who is confident enough to stand up for himself whilst respecting the rights of others. An assertive person is someone who has a positive mental attitude, self-belief and the confidence to express opinions. Someone who behaves assertively is keen to reach solutions to conflicts that give satisfaction to both sides. They will listen to others and do not impose their views on them. Their body language is confident and open, and their eye contact good.

However, assertive behaviour is not a natural form of behaviour for human beings. Humans are primed to behave in a certain way when faced with danger. Our natural reflexes mean that we will either want to run away (flight) or attack (fight). This is known as the flight

or fight response and can be translated into either behaving submissively (flight) or behaving aggressively (fight).

In today's society however, it is not acceptable for us to behave in this way because not only could we end up in trouble with the law but we could also damage our health. Behaving in an aggressive manner results in an increased heart rate, which can lead to high blood pressure, and therefore the possibility of heart attack and strokes. Behaving submissively leads to low self worth and a lack of confidence, which can result in greater exposure to viruses, infections and depression. And swinging between these two forms of behaviour will again result in poor health, as your body is continually preparing to fight or flight.

> **You need to adopt assertive behaviour, which not only benefits society but also leads to better health.**

Having said what assertiveness is let's just clarify the other forms of behaviour, submissive (flight) and aggressive (fight). As you read the following sections think of situations where you have been forced into doing something you don't want to do; how do you behave? Look at the descriptions and see whether either of these is typical of your response.

What does submissive behaviour mean?

Submissive behaviour means neglecting to defend your personal rights and beliefs. You put the rights of others before your own rights.

Are you behaving submissively?

I am always apologizing when I don't need to be

Yes☐ No☐

I have difficulty in making requests and go about it in a round about way   Yes☐ No☐

I am quietly spoken   Yes☐ No☐

I find it difficult holding eye contact with another person   Yes☐ No☐

I try not to be noticed in meetings or gatherings

Yes☐ No☐

I fidget unnecessarily   Yes☐ No☐

I have difficulty in speaking my mind   Yes☐ No☐

I don't like rocking the boat but prefer to keep things as they are, even if I don't like them   Yes☐   No☐

I have difficulty in expressing my feelings
                                                                    Yes☐   No☐

If you have answered mainly yes then your behaviour is submissive.

What makes us become submissive?

As mentioned before we can become submissive when we are under attack or even when we think we are going to be attacked. We can run away or withdraw into ourselves.

We can become submissive when faced with a bullying boss, partner, parent or someone else in an authoritative position.

Submissive individuals usually have low self-esteem, which can sometimes, but not always, be formed as a child. If you are told that you are useless, too fat, too tall, too thin, too clumsy this is how you will end up seeing yourself and your self worth will be dented.

I once met a lady who had been adopted and all throughout her childhood she had been told by her adoptive parents that she should be grateful they had taken her in, otherwise she would have ended up in a children's home. Subsequently this lady grew up believing she had to be grateful to everyone. She had very little self worth and was very submissive. Over the years I have had the pleasure of helping this lady, and seen her take control of her life, gain promotion and become much more assertive.

What does aggressive behaviour mean?

Aggressive behaviour means that you consider your rights and beliefs are more important than other people and you say so. Or you could behave in an underhand and manipulative manner to get your way.

Are you behaving aggressively?

I tend to deliver instructions and commands without consulting others   Yes❑ No❑

I like to be in control   Yes❑ No❑

I use a fair bit of sarcasm   Yes❑ No❑

When I am upset I can hold a grudge for a long time afterwards   Yes☐ No☐

When I am upset I fly off the handle too quickly
                                                                      Yes☐ No☐

If you have answered mainly yes, then you are behaving aggressively.

What makes us become aggressive?

Apart from being threatened or in danger of attack and adopting the fight response people become aggressive, or use aggression, because it gets them results. However, if an aggressive boss uses this behaviour regularly then he will very soon end up losing staff and especially those self-confident and assertive staff. The company will lose out in the long run by not being able to attract and retain bright confident individuals who contribute to its growth and future success.

Here's another example: the child screaming its head off in the supermarket is rewarded with a bag of sweets to keep it quiet – what message is this sending to that child? Yes, behave badly and you will be rewarded! The

child will carry on behaving badly because it has seen that this type of behaviour gets it want it wants.

People also behave aggressively because it gives them a sense of power and sometimes it covers up for their own insecurity.

There are some people who come across as being aggressive because they are trying too hard to assert themselves. Others end up acting aggressively because they do not have the education or the vocabulary to adequately express how they feel. The techniques described in the following chapters show how you can build assertiveness, project a more assertive and positive image, and how you can give an assertive response when dealing with difficult situations and people.

In summary

O   There are three main types of behaviour:

❑   Assertive
❑   Aggressive
❑   Submissive

O   Submissive means neglecting to defend your
     personal rights and beliefs

O   Aggressive means considering your rights and
     beliefs are more important than other people's

O   Assertive means standing up for your own rights
     without violating the rights of others

O   Being assertive means that you are confident
     enough to express your opinions, views and ideas
     and that you expect those opinions, views and
     ideas to be listened to

O   People behave aggressively because it gives them
     a sense of power and sometimes it covers up for
     their own insecurity

O   People behave aggressively if they are threatened

O   People become submissive when they are under
     attack or when they think they are going to be
     attacked

O   People become submissive when faced with a
     bullying boss, partner, parent or someone else in
     an authoritative position

○ Submissive individuals usually have low self-esteem

○ Being assertive can help us take control of our lives and give us a positive outlook.

Chapter 6

Self-Esteem

Self-esteem is forged at a very young age. It is the picture we form of ourselves through the eyes (and subsequently through the words and actions) of others: our parents, our relatives, our teachers and friends. It is the value we place upon ourselves.

To enable children to have a high self-esteem it is important that they experience rewards for good behaviour, that they are treated fairly and are heard and respected by their parents, teachers and other adults. The discipline they receive should be fair and not erratic.

Girls generally have naturally lower self-esteem than boys. This is mainly cultural and has been reinforced in the past and still is today in some cultures reflected by the status of women in society.

Some girls are uncomfortable in a superior role; they tend to underestimate their abilities and are prepared to accept second best. Girls also tend to set themselves lower goals in life than boys. They will repress their

successes when with boys. This can continue into adulthood and indeed into the workplace where women will often dismiss their successes with a modest 'It was nothing' even when they have spent a great deal of energy completing a very difficult and complex task successfully. Men are generally much better at telling others how well they have done or are doing.

Of course there are men, perhaps reading this book, who are suffering from this same low self-esteem and false modesty as their female counterparts, and there could be very confident women reading this book who have no difficulty in expressing their views, opinions and telling others of their successes. For others to appreciate you, you first need to appreciate yourself.

What do you like about yourself?

Take a piece of paper and for one minute write down what you like about yourself, for example: your sense of humour, your smile, your loyalty, your body, etc.

Did you struggle with this exercise? Are you still looking at a blank piece of paper?

In my experience many people find this exercise incredibly difficult. Yet, if I were to ask you what you

dislike about yourself you probably wouldn't stop scribbling for ten minutes. Why is it we are comfortable telling people what we don't like about ourselves or what we are 'useless' at rather than what we are good at? Why is it that when many of us are paid a compliment we shrug it off or throw it back in the other person's face?

Here's another example:

Boss: 'You did a good job on that report, Mary.'
Mary: 'It was nothing.'

And yet Mary had stayed late working to finish that report and had worked hard.

Friend: 'You look nice today, Joan. I like your suit.'
Joan: 'I've had this ages. I bought it from the charity shop.'

Let's rewind and try this again with the correct responses:

Boss: 'You did a good job on that report, Mary.'
Mary: 'Thank you. I worked hard on that and I am pleased with the results.'

Friend: 'You look nice today, Joan. I like your suit.'
Joan: 'Thank you.'

It takes a bit of practice but you *can* do it.

What are your strengths?

Exercise
In chapter four I asked you to complete a questionnaire on 'Getting to know yourself.' One of those questions was, 'What am I good at?' Now take another look at this question and your answers and write down what you consider to be your strengths. Often your strengths are those things that you are good at.

Again this can be a difficult exercise. If you really do not know what your strengths are then get someone who knows you to kick-start the process. Review the list together.

Not only do you need to take stock of your strengths but you may also need to draw others' attention to them. There could be occasions when you need to say 'I am good at that. It is a particular strength of mine. '

You cringe, why? Because it sounds too much like blowing your own trumpet. I am not talking about

bragging or boasting, but about being confident in yourself and your strengths.

There is another reason why we find this difficult and that is because our negative voice is saying, 'What if someone shoots me down and says I'm not good at this.' Don't worry they won't. But if they do then examine their motives. They could be envious of you, and putting you down makes them feel better. They could be afraid or insecure about their own strengths. If you are realistic about your strengths then hold fast to them, do not allow others to hi-jack them. Remember that positive voice, 'Yes, I am good at this.'

What if someone is unfairly criticizing you or constantly criticizing you? (Remember our list of negatives in chapter one). If you haven't taken stock of your strengths you will not be able to correct this unfair criticism either mentally or verbally.

There are many professions that have to put up with a great deal of public criticism: teachers for example who are constantly being told in the media that they are not good enough. Here, both good and bad teachers are lumped together. Even the most confident teachers can begin to develop a negative inner voice after being regularly subjected to this.

So how do you cope with constant criticizing? I examine this in more detail in chapter twelve, but first know your strengths, don't put yourself down, and don't allow others to put you down. Get a positive inner voice going and keep it going.

Here are some other ways to help you handle negativity and criticism from other people.

1. List your strengths/positive assets/what you like about yourself.

2. Put this on a board near your desk or in the bathroom at home or anywhere you can see it

3. Look at it every morning

4. Say your positive traits out loud to yourself

5. When you are feeling negative, or someone has said something negative to you, re visit this list and remind yourself of your good points.

In summary

O   Self-esteem is forged at a very young age

O   Self-esteem is the picture we form of ourselves through the eyes, words and actions of others

O   Girls generally have naturally lower self-esteem than boys

O   For others to appreciate you, you need to appreciate yourself

O   You need to take stock of your strengths and weaknesses

O   If you are realistic about your strengths then hold fast to them, do not allow others to hi jack them

O   Say your positive traits out loud

O   When you are feeling negative, or someone has said something negative to you, then re visit your strengths and remind yourself of your good points

Chapter 7

Projecting a confident image

Image is important. The wrong image can blow your credibility before you even open your mouth. Projecting the right image can make you feel and act more positively and therefore make others act more positively towards you.

The image that you give out is based on:
55% See, 38% Hear, 7% Word.

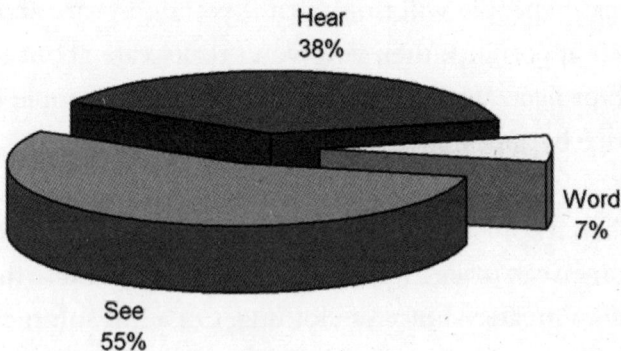

The 55% of what we see is made up of our appearance and our body language.

Appearance

How you look, your clothes and your personal grooming are important. If you look dishevelled then people will think you are disorganized and scatterbrained. If you need to communicate a serious message to someone then you will need to look authoritative otherwise you won't be taken seriously. You will also need to speak with a clear and positive voice and communicate through confident body language.

If you have an important business meeting to attend and your little boy has just been sick on your best suit, or you haven't had time to have your hair cut and styled this is communicating that you're disorganized or lazy because people will think that if you don't care about your appearance then you won't really care about the job/project. Wrong, yes, but unfortunately people do judge by appearances.

When it comes to deciding what to wear for the office, women can make more mistakes than men because they have a greater choice of clothing. On a hot summer's day women begin to strip off the layers of clothing and start wearing sandals, T-shirts, flowing skirts and skimpy dresses. This can damage a woman's credibility, as well as be a distraction to the men!

There is a saying:

**The more flesh you show the less
credible you are.**

At work, as a woman, if you dress in flounces and frills,
wear pastel colours and lots of makeup, and speak in a
little girl voice, it is unlikely that you will be taken
seriously.

If dressed for the disco or nightclub then again I doubt
you will be taken seriously in the workplace.

In some organisations the dress code is more relaxed,
so that's fine. Both men and women need to be aware
that clothes say a lot about personality. Be comfortable
with what you wear, but at the same time be conscious
of the impression you are giving out.

When deciding on what to wear ask yourself the
following questions:

O   What is the message I wish to communicate?
O   Who am I going to see or meet?
O   What should I wear?

If your intention is to build rapport with someone then dressing to suit the situation and person will make them feel more at ease with you. We've all had experiences where we have turned up for an event wearing the wrong clothes and we know how uncomfortable that makes us feel. Make sure you don't make the person you are communicating with feel that way about you.

> **Use clothes to assert yourself
> and to build rapport.**

Choosing the right type of clothes

How do you feel when you put on your jogging pants, or a pair of jeans or shorts? Relaxed, comfortable? How do you feel when you put on a dinner suit or an evening dress? The clothes you wear make you feel differently, they make you walk differently, they change your body language and therefore the messages you are sending out to others.

For work getting the right clothes is important for how you feel, act and perform. You may have little choice in

the matter because your occupation requires you to put on a uniform. But even if you are not required to wear a formal uniform we still have a uniform of sorts for most jobs i.e. the suit for office wear.

There are now some companies that operate a dress down day on a Friday. However, some people feel uncomfortable about this and research has shown that performance can drop on the days when people come into work in a more causal form of dress. This has led to some companies abolishing this rule, and sometimes at the request of its employees. Some men wouldn't feel dressed if they didn't wear a tie to work, others would hate it and often their jobs don't require them to do so.

Those who work from home are often advised to dress as if they are out to work to enhance their professionalism and boost their confidence.

The no uniform day in schools is dreaded by most teachers who will very quickly tell you that they make the pupils unruly.

So there is something to be said for dressing the part to boost your confidence and to project a more positive

image. This doesn't mean wearing the power suit it just means wearing what makes you feel good and is appropriate for the task, you wouldn't wear an evening dress to do the vacuuming or change a tap, and you wouldn't wear your best suit to unblock the lavatory! That may just be common sense but then there is no substitute for that.

Whatever your size or shape, male or female, be aware of body shape and the styles of clothes that emphasize this and that suit you.

Learn to play up your strengths and down your weaknesses. What colours enhance you, what colours drain you? Take advice from a colour or style consultant if necessary.

And remember:

> **You never get a second chance to make a first impression!**

Giving a Presentation

If you need to give a presentation at work then you will need to project authority. You should dress according to the audience you are addressing. This doesn't mean to say if the audience looks causal and scruffy you should also. On the contrary you should always be presentable.

For a more formal presentation a darker suit will aid authority and you can always wear it with a coloured scarf or tie if you wish to slightly soften this image. Always check the fit of the suit when buttoned. When you are standing, and giving a formal presentation, your suit should be buttoned up.

For the more informal presentation where you want people to open up, for example a training seminar, staff meeting or creative thinking session you can wear less severe colours and styles, and can use brighter colours and patterns. But don't bombard your audience with too many colours or too bold a pattern, you will overwhelm them and distract them from your essential purpose, which is to convey information.

Self Image

Your self-image, how you see yourself, is vital to your well-being.

If you are constantly comparing yourself with others and find yourself lacking then you are putting yourself down.

For example you see or meet someone and that negative voice inside you says, 'She looks nice, I wish I looked like that,' or 'He's got a good physique I wish mine was like that.' Can you see how you come out the poorer in this exchange? You might continue with this inner dialogue adding, 'I will never be as slim or attractive as that. It's not fair. There's nothing I can do about it. No one will like me. I don't know why I bother…' If dialogues like this are going through your head can you hear how negative they are? How are you going to feel? Yes, pretty miserable. And what is your body language going to do? Yes, be slumped and negative.

So what do you need to do about it? Let's rewind and correct this negative inner voice:

'She looks good. I am different to her and I look good too.'

OK, so it may seem strange to you, and you may not believe it at first, but remember the power of the brain. By stating this to yourself you are conditioning your brain into a positive response. This will have an effect on your body language, which will be more positive, and in turn will send positive messages back to your brain.

Value your individuality. Revisit your checklist on the good points you came up with earlier. Say them to yourself. Tell yourself what you have going for yourself.

Are you presenting yourself as a stereotype?

Do you model yourself on a television personality or pick a ready-made image off the shelf of someone you admire or even envy? This can be just as damaging for you. How can you be like another person, you are you, you are unique, value that uniqueness and enjoy it.

In summary

O   Image is important; the wrong image can blow
      your credibility

O   How you are perceived plays an important part
      in communication

O   The image that you give out is based on:

         55%   See
         38%   Hear
         7%   Word

O   If you look dishevelled people will think you are
      disorganized and scatterbrained

O   Your clothes say a lot about your personality

O   Dress to suit your personality but at the same time
      be aware of the impression you are giving out

O   When deciding what to wear ask:

         ❑   What is the message I wish to
              communicate?
         ❑   Who am I going to see or meet?
         ❑   What should I wear?

O   If you are constantly comparing yourself with others and find yourself lacking then you are putting yourself down

O   Value your individuality

O   Use clothes to assert yourself and to change how you feel

O   Learn to play up your strengths and down your weaknesses

O   Remember: you never get a second chance to make a first impression!

O   For a formal presentation you will need to project authority

O   For an informal presentation you can wear less severe colours and styles and can use brighter colours and patterns

Chapter 8

Body Language

How you project yourself through your body language is vitally important. You may be saying (speaking) the right words but if your body language is communicating another message then it is this message that your recipient/s will hear.

Non-verbal signals are said to be at least four and a half times as effective as verbal signals, and facial expressions eight times as powerful as the words used. We look at someone a third of the time we are talking to them, and this look can convey anything from boredom and irritation to enthusiasm and liking.

You can also enhance the image you project and your feelings of self-confidence by deliberately using more positive body language. As stated in chapter one positive body language will send positive messages to your brain, which in turn will send even more positive messages back to your body language. People will pick up on this and will therefore act more positively towards you.

Your Handshake

Your handshake can say a great deal about you. A firm dry handshake reveals confidence, professionalism and status. If you have a weak handshake, even if you are not a weak person, it will give out the wrong impression. So what is your handshake like? Try shaking hands with someone you know and ask them for their honest opinion. If you need to firm it up then practice it.

Women need to give what I call the man's handshake. Take the whole hand and not just the fingertips. Grasp the hand and ensure your handshake is firm. Sometimes women are unsure whether or not to shake hands. This is because the handshake is essentially a male form of greeting. However, there are now many women in business and therefore women too need to shake hands not only with men but also with other women. If in doubt always offer your hand first and invariably the other person will take it.

What the handshake can reveal

The double clutch handshake is often referred to as the politician's handshake. It is where someone wants to touch more of you to connect with you. It is also a dominant gesture. This person is saying to you that

they are in charge of the interchange between you. If you do not wish to accept this then put your other hand on top of theirs. It may feel a little funny but it is perfectly acceptable and communicates to the other person that you can be equally forceful even if you don't feel it!

The at arms length handshake, stiff and fully extended is telling others to keep away. This communicates a superior or aloof personality.

The person who holds onto your hand longer than necessary is giving out a dominant body language signal. This person is saying, 'I am not going to let go of you until I feel like it because I am in charge here.' There is very little you can do about this except tighten your pressure and keep your eye contact on the other person, smiling at the same time.

The vice like grip again is a dominant gesture or indicates a dominant personality. In this case return the pressure and maintain good eye contact with the other person.

When you shake hands take the whole hand with firmness, smile and make direct eye contact.

The First Impression

As I've already mentioned you never get a second chance to make a first impression so if you would like to exude confidence, even if you don't feel that confident, then you can by getting your appearance right, and by communicating the correct body language. The first body language signals are:

- handshake
- eye contact
- smile

When you meet someone walk up to them with your hand outstretched, smile at them and give them good strong eye contact. Take their hand in a firm grasp (but not too firm) with your elbow tucked into your waist, keep your body posture upright and your shoulders back and make a pleasant opening remark – there is nothing wrong with saying, 'How do you do?' 'Pleased to meet you,' Hello I'm …(give your name)' or all three – 'How do you do I'm (name). I'm pleased to meet you?'

Walking confidently into a room

Making an entrance may not be your style but equally cringing and hugging the escape hatch (the door) should not be either. Most people find walking into a crowded room, or a room full of strangers, daunting, but you **can do it.**

How?

First have you got the right inner voice – a positive one?

Let's examine what is being said inside your head: 'I'm dreading this. I wish I didn't have to do this. Everyone's going to be looking at me and laughing at me. I won't know anyone there. It's going to be awful.'

Do you **hear** that faulty negative inner voice? Tell it to **STOP**

❑ **Hear it**
❑ **Recognize it**

Next we need to **Challenge** it. Will *everyone* be looking at you? Why will people be laughing at you? Of course they won't.

Change the negative voice
to a positive one

For Example

'There will be others who will be equally nervous. I won't be alone. I can handle this. No one's going to eat me. It's not life threatening. I can deal with this.'

Get that positive dialogue going inside your head, tell yourself that you can do it, set your shoulders back, take stock of your positive qualities, and walk in. Keep your body posture upright but not taut; scan the room for a friendly face and head for it. I usually look for the person standing alone (there is always one) and make a beeline for them. Using the greeting mentioned previously I might follow this up with 'I don't know anyone here, do you?' And the conversation can start to flow. Alternatively, if there is a queue for coffee or lunch I will join it and start talking to either the person in front of me or behind me, the common topic being the queue or the event we're both attending.

Visualization

One technique that I find works well if you are feeling nervous and that is to recall an occasion in your life when you felt very confident and happy. This could be

when you passed your driving test, or an exam, how did you feel then? Elated, confident, happy. What do you think your body language was like? Confident, positive, good. Visualize that moment again in your mind and that will evoke the same feelings and positive body language.

Personal Space

Personal space is the space around us that we feel comfortable in. We only allow those close to us to invade that space. If others do so uninvited then we feel threatened by them and wish to step back. Make sure you are not invading other people's personal space. Different cultures have different distances so be aware of this. British people are usually comfortable at a distance of about three feet.

Meetings

Where to sit
If you want recognition at a meeting always sit within good eye contact of the decision maker (who may not always be the chair).

To mitigate a confrontation sit next to the challenger. It is far more difficult to attack from the side. Avoid sitting directly opposite the person.

If you are a junior, or new participant, wait to be told where to sit.

To avoid attention sit in a blind spot for the chair, that is where it is physically difficult for them to see you and wear your most neutral outfit with no special accessories.

Positive body language signals

○ Try linking your hands together as though to form a steeple. This prevents you making nervous mannerisms

○ If you have a table in front of you, with your hands linked, you stake out territory for yourself, this suggests confidence and self-possession

○ Stillness suggests ease and comfort in a situation, especially the ability to keep hands and feet still and relaxed

○ Gestures showing open palms of hands demonstrate openness and confidence

○ Sitting asymmetrical demonstrates confidence in taking space

O   Leaning forward indicates interest, but it can also indicate that you are putting in quite a lot of effort and seeking involvement at the expense of your self possession therefore it can lower your status

O   Stand comfortably with your hands and arms relaxed at your side

Further impressive body language signals

O   Sit upright and alert

O   Keep your eyes on the speaker

O   Take notes in a meeting, not constantly, but key points

O   Turn your body to the speaker/chair

O   When listening keep your body open, arms leaning forward on the table, hands gently folded. Relaxed.

O   Use open gestures.

O   Smile, use humour to alleviate tension

Negative body language signals to avoid

O   Nervous mannerisms, nail biting, finger and foot
     tapping, playing with hair, or adjusting clothing,
     smoothing eyebrows

O   Playing with objects and personal effects;
     wedding rings, pencils etc. often indicates tension

O   Pointing at people, waving your fist, thumping
     the table, shows aggression and tension

O   Touching the face is associated with negative
     emotions: guilt, self doubt, irritation

O   Touching the chin and mouth: doubt, reluctance
     to speak or accept what is being said

O   Touching the nose: said to be an indication of
     lying

O   Touching the eye: not liking what you are seeing
     or not wanting to see any further.

O   Touching the ears: not liking what you are hearing

Don't

○   Slouch

○   Look down at notes, out of window, at the ceiling

○   Doodle

○   Physically turn away

○   Fold your arms tightly across your body which says you're not listening

○   Growl, frown, or use cynical expressions.

For more on image and body language read *The Easy Step by Step Guide to Communicating with More Confidence* by Pauline Rowson.

In summary

○   How you project yourself through your body language is vitally important

○   You can also enhance your self confidence by deliberately using more positive body language

○ A firm dry handshake reveals confidence, professionalism and status

○ If you have a weak handshake, even if you are not a weak person, it will give out the wrong impression

○ Take the whole hand with firmness, smile and make direct eye contact

○ Make sure you are not invading other's personal space

Chapter 9

It's what you say and how you say it

You can project a positive image and increase your feelings of being positive by using the power of language and expressing yourself with clarity: speaking in a strong, steady voice neither shouting nor mumbling.

Exercise
Record a conversation with a friend or colleague then play it back. How does your voice sound?

Do you need to change the way you speak? I am not talking about accents here (accents are fine as long as others can understand you) but about the clarity of your voice. To sound enthusiastic as well as interesting vary the pace of your voice. Keep your head up and your voice box open. Practice giving good direct eye contact as you talk to the other person.

If your voice is too loud or you speak too fast then practice speaking more softly and slowly. To build rapport you need to match the pace and pitch of the other person. Be aware of how others speak and adapt your style accordingly.

Watch your language

Example

John wanted to convince his boss that he needed two more people on his team. He had the facts and figures to back this up but when he met the boss he kept adding in little phrases like:

'Do you know what I mean?'

'You know?'

'Can you understand what I'm saying?'

'Actually'

'In fact'

'Basically'

At the end of his case the boss was far from convinced. John was weakening the power of his words by using statements that were unnecessary and in some cases he put question marks at the end of them. This makes John sound as if he is constantly seeking permission for his arguments. If you keep qualifying what you are saying, and checking that others approve, you will not sound confident. I have used a male in the above example but unfortunately women do this far more than men.

Exercise

Do you pepper your conversation with unnecessary phrases and words? Return to your recording – what unnecessary phrases do you use?

Are you guilty of using phrases that put you down? For example:

'I'm hopeless at this.'

'You know me, I seem to be useless at...'

'I can't seem to...'

Another thing we sometimes do is apologize when we don't need to, for example:

'I'm sorry but I thought you said…'
(he did why should you apologize).

'I'm terribly sorry, I didn't really mean to...'

'I'm very sorry to bother you.'

'I hope you don't really mind but would it be all right if...'

'Excuse me please but can we...'

> ## To project a more assertive image
> ## practice assertive words using 'I'
> ## rather than 'You'

For example:

> I believe
> My idea is
> I would like
> I prefer
> I feel
> I think
> As I see it...
> My view is.

'I'd like to change the date of the meeting', instead of, 'It would be a good idea to change the date of the meeting.'

Use co-operative words like 'Let's' and 'We could.'

For example:

> 'Let's look for a way to overcome this.'
> 'How can we get round this?'
> 'Shall we?'

Make your statements brief and to the point. For example:

'I'd like to get started this week.'

From this it is clear what you want. By contrast long rambling statements confuse the other person leaving them unclear about what you want: 'I thought you might like to er... um... well....'

Use questions to find out thoughts, opinions and wants of others.

'How does that fit in with your plans?'
'What will this involve...?'
'What are your thoughts on...?'

Making requests

You don't have to justify yourself for making requests, for example: 'I wouldn't normally ask but the car's broken down and my husband is in bed with the flu, I know it's out of your way but just this once, would you mind awfully giving me a lift?' Phew!

When making requests of others be direct and short but not curt. For example, 'I'm without the car

tomorrow could you give me a lift into work, John?'
Or 'I would like that report by the end of the week,
Anne.' 'I would like you in by eight o'clock, Jamie.'

You can give a reason for your request if you think it
will help but be sure it's genuine and keep it brief. And
if John in our example above says he can't give you a
lift into work then respect his right to say 'no'. Don't
take it personally, and don't flatter or argue him into
changing his mind; that is aggressive behaviour.

With a work request give more information and seek
clarification. Find out why the other person is refusing.
If the answer is still no then put your energy into joint
problem-solving rather than persuading the other
person to meet your request as originally outlined.
Don't sell your request with flattery or tempting
benefits. For example:

> 'Linda, you're just the person', or 'Bob, this is
> right up your street. I'm sure you'll be interested.'

Don't play on people's friendships or good nature
either. For example:

> 'Be a pal and get this done by lunchtime.'

Refusing requests

Responding assertively

Let's now look at an example of how we can respond assertively to a request that we would like to refuse.

You agree to pick up a colleague on your way to work knowing this means getting up an ungodly hour, taking the children to their grandparents earlier than usual and having to go slightly out of your way. This means you will get stuck in the traffic jam by the industrial estate. But you say yes, and then make yourself ill, and get cross with everyone around you because you are busting a gut to do it.

You have given into a request when you would have preferred not to. In this example you have behaved submissively. So how should you have dealt with this request in an assertive way?

Your assertive response to the request should have been:

> 'Sorry, Jane, I can't give you a lift as it is out of my way. I could pick you up on route though by the cinema.'

You have suggested a much more convenient place to pick up Jane, which does not mean you have to go to the ends of the earth to accommodate her. In all likelihood she'll probably say, 'Don't bother, I'll ask my boyfriend. He'll bring me. I just thought I'd try you first.'

The assertive response sees you standing up for yourself. I could go further and say that you don't really have to apologize or give a reason (though some people will find this difficult). You could simply say. 'I can't Jane, but I could pick you up on route by the cinema.'

How to say 'no'

It is only a little word, two letters – that's all. And yet it is one of the hardest words to use. Saying 'no' to requests is something many of us find difficult, and even when we do say 'no' we can often feel guilty. Remember you have the right to say 'no.' Listed below are some techniques to help you cope with this little word and how to use it.

Keep your reply short

When refusing a request keep your reply short but not abrupt. You can simply say, 'I'd prefer not to,' or 'I'd rather not,' or 'No, I'm not happy to...' Avoid using 'I can't' phrases if possible as these can start sounding like excuses.

With short replies you need to slow down, speak steadily and with warmth otherwise it can sound abrupt.

Buy yourself some time

If you are not used to saying 'no', and find refusing requests difficult, then buy yourself some time. Don't commit yourself straight away. And don't agree to anything you are even faintly concerned about.

You can buy time by asking for clarification or more information. For example:

> 'What detail does this report have to go into?'

> 'I need to think/look into this. I'll get back to you in ten minutes/half an hour.'

> 'I need to check with my diary/husband/ partner/ colleague. I'll get back to you later today/in half an hour.'

> 'Bob, I need to check on my schedule before agreeing to help with this project. I will ring you tomorrow.'

Then you can get back to the person making the request using some of the advice below.

Get all the facts

Don't allow yourself to be caught doing something if your reason for being involved is still vague. Ask for specifics: time, location, how long will you be needed, what is the exact cost, when is the information due?

Use the person's name

An assertive response would also be to acknowledge the person who is making the request by name, for example 'Thank you, Anne, but I'm not ready to take my lunch break yet.'

Don't blame others

Don't put the blame for refusing the request onto others; identify yourself with the decision. For example: 'I'm not prepared to bend the rules on this,' rather than, 'Senior management wouldn't want to change it.' 'I'd prefer not to go to the party' rather than 'My husband wouldn't like it.'

Give a reason

Give the real reason for refusing. However, sometimes, if you are not used to refusing, or you think you may offend the other person, the little white lie is acceptable.

If the requester becomes persistent then repeat your refusal adding the reason if you didn't give it first time.

Leave it out if you gave it first time. Don't search for better reasons.

Know your limits

When refusing work requests it is best if you know beforehand your own limits (workload, time restraints) and your priorities, so that you can put the refusal into context. You can say, 'I'm unable to do that now, Mary, but I'll make it a priority first thing in the morning,' or 'I will tackle that task as soon as I have this proposal finished.'

In summary

◯ You can project a positive image and increase your feelings of being positive by using the power of language and changing the way you express yourself

◯ Practice speaking with clarity

◯ Talk in a strong, steady voice neither shouting nor mumbling

◯ Practice giving good direct eye contact as you talk to the other person

○ If your voice is too loud or fast then practice speaking more softly and slowly

○ To build rapport you need to match the pace and pitch of the other person

○ Be aware of how others speak and adapt your style accordingly

○ Don't apologize when you don't need to

○ Practice assertive words: 'I' not 'You'

○ Practice co-operative words:
  ❑ 'Let's'
  ❑ 'We could'

○ Make your statements brief and to the point

○ Use questions to find out thoughts, opinions and wants of others

○ Avoid apologetic phrases

○ When making requests of others be direct and short but not curt

O Don't take a 'no' personally.

O Don't sell your request with flattery or tempting benefits

O Don't play on people's friendships or good nature

O When refusing a request keep your reply short but not abrupt

O Don't commit yourself straight away – buy yourself some time before answering

O Ask for clarification or more information if you need it

O If the requester becomes persistent then repeat your refusal adding the reason if you didn't give it first time

Chapter 10

Handling unproductive feelings

A positive inner voice

I have already mentioned the importance of having a positive inner voice (see chapter two). I now want to look at this in more detail. Getting the right inner voice can help you to become more assertive and therefore handle those difficult situations and people more confidently. If you don't get this right then it is likely that you will behave aggressively or submissively. Let's look at a couple of examples to illustrate this.

Example 1
You are on your way to speak to a client who has complained about your organisation's services. He has previously taken up a lot of your time with similar complaints. He is very difficult and you find handling him tough.

This might be the dialogue that is going on inside your head:

> 'It's typical of people like him. He's a nuisance.
> He's always complaining. He's no right to take
> up my time like this.'

Your feelings are of frustration, anger, and impatience.
Therefore, if you don't correct this negative inner voice,
your behaviour will reflect those feelings and you will
behave aggressively towards the client. He in turn will
pick up on this behaviour and you have a clash and a
no win situation.

Example 2
You are about to go to a job interview.

This might be the dialogue that is going on inside your
head:

> 'This is going to be really tough. I'm so nervous.
> I hate job interviews. What if they ask me
> questions I can't answer? I know I'll blush/
> stammer and make a fool of myself. I'll try and
> get it over with as quickly as possible. Besides I
> won't get the job anyway, there'll be far more
> qualified people attending.'

Your feelings are worry, anxiety, panic, and helplessness.
You will stumble over your words, gabble, and change

your mind too easily when questioned. You will generally look incompetent even though you might not be so. Will you get that job? No, of course you won't.

If you think you are going to fail then you will because your body language will reflect that and you will be giving out negative signals, which others will pick up. Just as positive people attract other positive people so the opposite applies.

So taking the last example we need to hear that faulty inner voice, recognize it, challenge it and change it to a positive inner voice.

So the positive inner dialogue could be:

> 'This may be a tough interview but I can handle it. I am good at my job and I have a great deal of experience to offer. These are my strengths, which I can convey to the interview panel. I have prepared well and am looking forward to the challenge. If I am asked questions I can't answer then I will say so with confidence and demonstrate what I do know.'

Think positive. Say these positive things aloud to yourself in the car, in your house, in the garden. They

will reflect in your body language. Walk into that room confidently with a smile on your face and give all the members of the panel sweeping eye contact.

It may take practice but remember the old proverb 'practice makes perfect.'

Exercise
Now look at the example on page 117 and have a go at correcting that inner voice and changing it from a negative one to a positive one.

How others influence you

Of course other people may influence you and cause negative thoughts to flood into your mind. You can be influenced by what they say and how they say it, that is the content of what they are saying and their behaviour.

Example
You need to introduce a new procedure to your team at the staff meeting. Jane is the most difficult member of your team and always puts up some objections. You just know she will this time.

Before you go into this meeting you need to get the right inner voice.

'OK, so Jane is usually difficult but I can deal with her. I have good reasons for introducing these changes and I can make my point assertively.'

In the meeting Jane challenges your statement about increased efficiency coming from these changes. She says, 'Oh come on, that's rubbish! If you do that there will be enormous problems; we'll never get the system back on line. Remember the last changes you introduced weren't particularly brilliant!'

Jane has acted aggressively. Her attack seems to have been personal, and like many who use aggressive statements there are exaggerations in her dialogue: 'that's rubbish,' 'enormous problems,' 'never.'

Your response to being attacked like this might be to get angry back; 'I'm in charge, Jane, so just do as you're told,' or to run away, 'Well, maybe I should look at it again.'

You have responded either aggressively or submissively. Instead you should make sure your inner dialogue is positive, don't take it personally: remember you have good reasons for introducing these changes and tell yourself this. Your assertive response to Jane should be something along the lines of:

'Jane, I believe the changes will improve the overall efficiency; we will start implementing them in a week's time. In the meantime if you, or anyone else, has any constructive suggestions to make on the changes, then I am willing to look at them. Could you get these to me in writing, backed up with evidence, by Thursday morning?'

Let's examine this statement in detail for evidence that it is assertive:

Use of the person's name: Jane

Use of the assertive statement; 'I believe'

Willingness to look at other suggestions and listen to people but assertion that my decision will stand if this is not backed up.

Let's look another response to your announcement. Instead of Jane being aggressive, another colleague, Simon, behaves submissively. He says, 'Well, we do have a lot on at the moment and... er... these changes are bound to take up some of our time. But I suppose we'll try and manage somehow.'

If you don't maintain your assertiveness you could feel guilty about putting more work on Simon's shoulders and therefore behave submissively yourself. 'Just do the best you can Simon,' which means that nothing is going to happen.

Or you could feel cross that Simon is always whining and therefore behave aggressively towards him. 'For goodness sake, Simon, just do it if you want to keep your job in this company.'

So what should your assertive response be?

> 'Simon, you obviously have concerns about implementing these changes, perhaps you could let me know what they are and we can look at them in more detail.'

Influencing through past behaviour

Sometimes you are influenced through past behaviour. For example there is a person who always gets your back up. You only have to hear their voice on the telephone, or see them walking towards you, and that negative voice pops up. 'Oh no, it's Margaret again, she's such a pain in the neck. I can't stand that woman; she makes my blood boil.'

If this is the dialogue in your head then how are you going to behave towards Margaret? Either aggressively, getting your attack in first, or submissively, running away from her or backing down.

So what should your inner voice be saying? A positive inner voice should go something like this:

> 'Margaret is a difficult lady to deal with but I can handle her. I can keep calm.'

And if you do feel yourself losing it with Margaret then don't beat yourself over the head about it; say to yourself,

> 'Next time I'll do better with Margaret. I'll keep calm longer.'

In summary

O Positive people attract other positive people

O Think positive; convert negative dialogues into positive ones

O Other people may influence you and cause negative thoughts – make sure your inner voice is positive.

Chapter 11

Tackling the difficult situation or person

Dealing with angry people and handling conflict is never easy. We need to express ourselves without losing our temper or bursting into tears.

Having the positive inner voice as mentioned in the previous chapter is a good starting point. But you may need more than this. Very often we lose our temper or behave submissively because we don't know how to express our emotions. We need a framework for this and the four part statement (discussed on page 126) gives us this. This is an excellent technique when you are faced with someone who is behaving in a way that you find unacceptable.

Recognize this scenario?

At work David has upset you because he keeps shouting at you and throwing work at you just as you are about to leave for home. You feel pressurized into staying late to do the work. Then when you have finished it you often find that David has already gone home. You go

home and complain bitterly to your long-suffering partner who tells you that you should stand up for yourself and tell David to stick his job. You then shout at your partner accusing him of not understanding and you end up arguing! Or you go to bed thinking it over and over in your head, rehearsing imaginary conversations. You wake up at three o'clock in the morning worrying about it, then you go into work the next day tired and it starts all over again. Whilst you are worrying yourself sick David has had a lovely night's sleep and carries on as normal.

You tell everyone what the problem is but you don't tell David – why? Because you're worried you might lose your temper or burst into tears, or you might lose your job. The only way to change David's behaviour is to tell him about it and this is where the four part statement comes in.

The four part statement

- ❏ **When you do/say that**
- ❏ **I feel**
- ❏ **Because**
- ❏ **I'd rather/prefer**

This excellent technique allows you to reason things out in your own mind, and can also give you a framework for tackling these difficult or delicate situations.

Let's look at our previous example and see how it can apply.

When you do/say that: what is it that David is doing? He is shouting at you and giving you work too late in the day for you to complete on time.

I feel: how do you feel? Angry, frustrated, upset.

Because: why? Because you can't complete the work on time, because you have other commitments outside of work that are important to you, because you don't like being shouted at – who does?

I'd rather/prefer: what do you want to change? What would you rather happen? That David stops shouting at you and gives you work on time.

In this case I would also go a step further and ask myself why David is not giving me the work on time? Is it because he's a poor time manager? Is he disorganized or inefficient? Perhaps he can't cope with his job, or

could he be under pressure and that is why he's shouting at you? That doesn't excuse him but it helps me to understand that it's not personal, and if he doesn't change his behaviour then his health could suffer.

My first tip to you is that when something upsetting occurs don't react immediately. Take time out to think it through using the four part statement technique. Be specific about what is making you angry. What solution would you like? Write it down if it helps you. Say it aloud. Then, when you are ready, ask to see David in private. When you speak to him, stick to the point and the present, don't drag other facts into the conversation, or what happened last week, last month or last year.

Pause, breathe, don't rush in. Using the four part statement that you have rehearsed here's what you might say:

> 'David, when you give me this work late in the afternoon, and insist that it is done before I leave work, I feel very frustrated and uncomfortable because I like to do a professional job but can't because of the lack of time. I am unable to stay late because of my other commitments. In future I would like the work earlier in the day so that I may complete it for you.'

You could suggest a time that you and David could meet up to discuss what is urgent and non urgent, and help him prioritize. Or you could go on to suggest that you both sit down and see if you can plan the workload better.

But what happens if David isn't reasonable and this is the answer that you get?

> 'Don't be ridiculous, Mary. How do I know what I'm going to be able to give you and when? You'll just have to stay late. Where is your commitment to this company? There are plenty of others who would like your job.'

Ouch!!! What a bully. Do you really want to continue working for someone who behaves like this and doesn't appreciate you? Anyway, the right way to deal with this kind of response is to hold your ground. Keep your body language upright but not too stiff, keep your eye contact on him, look and sound assertive even if your knees are knocking and your heart is pounding, and repeat the final part of your four part statement:

You: 'I'd prefer it if you gave me the work earlier.'

David: 'You know I can't do that. I've just told you.'

You: 'I'd prefer to have the work earlier.'

David may go off in a huff, still moaning at you but he will think again before giving you the work too late. If he does continue you need to once again assert yourself and say:

> 'I am unable to do this now. I will make it my priority in the morning.'

And do so. David should get the message unless he is a real bully then you will need to examine your job description, log the incidents and get a witness to them and talk to the manager above David, or the human resources manager depending on your organization's grievance policy and procedure.

Let's look at another scenario. This is one that happened to me many years ago.

My boss took great delight in making personal remarks about me, my figure, my clothes, appearance etc. I didn't mind these at first but as time went on they began to get more personal and he started making these remarks in front of colleagues and clients. I had to put a stop to them. So I approached him and said:

'When you make those personal remarks about me, Jim, I feel very uncomfortable because I find it humiliating. In future I'd rather you didn't make these remarks.'

My boss was extremely apologetic. He didn't realize they upset me. He thought he was treating me as 'one of the boys' (men have a much more ribbing style than women, and I was working in a male dominated environment). From that moment onwards he stopped and things were fine between us.

But what if he hadn't been reasonable? His response could have been:

'What's wrong, can't you take a joke? I'm only teasing you. You women are so sensitive – if you can't hack it you shouldn't be here.'

DON'T justify your reasons – if you do you'll start to dig a big hole for yourself and probably end up apologizing when you shouldn't (submissive behaviour). Simply repeat the outcome you want:

'In future I'd rather you didn't make these remarks.'

Exercise

Try the response to the following scenario before looking at the answer.

A colleague from another department is constantly criticizing your decisions and your work by making snide remarks behind your back. You need to tackle the issue. You meet her and say...

Answer:

> 'Mary, I am aware that you are making remarks about me to others. When you do this, I feel annoyed/disappointed because you are undermining my authority (or questioning my ability, views and judgments). In future, if you have anything to say, I'd rather/prefer you say it to me direct and then we can look at the issue or deal with it together.'

Again you may get pressure from Mary: 'Who told you I was talking about you?' Mary becomes defensive and aggressive. Don't get drawn into arguing about the rights and wrongs of who told you. Simply repeat the outcome you want: 'If you have anything to say I'd rather you say it to me direct.'

In summary

○ Be specific about what is making you angry

○ If you can, deal with it there and then, if not shortly afterwards

○ Stick to the point and the present don't drag other facts into it or what happened last month or last year

○ Chose the right time and place – out of the public gaze would be best

○ Think the situation through to the conclusion you want

○ Map out what you want before hand. Write it down if it helps you

○ Practice the four part statement:
  ❑ When you say/do
  ❑ I feel
  ❑ Because
  ❑ I'd rather/prefer

O   Know your own advantages but don't underestimate theirs

O   Work out what is your last best option – the bottom line

O   Be mentally prepared for ultimatums

O   Be prepared to be put under pressure

O   Deal with the problem and not the person

O   Concentrate on the main issues, don't allow yourself to get sidetracked

Chapter 12

Handling put downs and criticism

Put downs or sarcasm can be extremely difficult to deal with. They are a form of aggressive behaviour. They are used to make you question your decisions and to belittle you.

So how do you deal with them?

There are two ways. One is to take them seriously and question the put down. The other is to state your views or your position.

Depending on who is giving the put down, why, and the circumstances in which it is intended there is another way of dealing with them and that is to laugh at them, or treat them with humour, but beware you don't become sarcastic back.

Let's take a couple of examples:

Put down:

>   'It's all right for you part timers you don't have the same responsibilities.'

Answer:

>   'I may work part time but I also take the responsibilities of my job seriously.'

You have accepted the first part of the put down statement because it is a fact but not the second part. You have asserted that you take your responsibilities seriously. You have stated your position/view.

Put down:

>   'You working mothers are all the same – no commitment.'

Answer:

>   'I am a working mother, but I take my job and its commitments very seriously.'

Again you can't dispute the fact that you are a working mother but you assert that you take your commitments very seriously.

In some cases you may not have to acknowledge the fact, i.e. the first part of the put down but simply state your position or view. For example:

Put down:

> 'Of course you don't have the same pressures as me.'

Answer:

> 'We all have different pressures.'

Put down:

> 'You don't really believe that do you?'

Answer:

> 'Yes, I do.'

Put down:

> 'That was a *stupid* decision.'

Answer:

> 'I accept the decision was wrong, but I don't accept it was stupid.'

The word 'stupid' is the put down here.

The other option is to question the put down. For example:

Put down:
> 'I expect *you've* got plenty of spare time.'

Answer:
> 'Really, what makes you say that?

Here you have answered the put down with a question.

You may know someone who always seems to come up with just the right answer to a put down, a witty quip that makes you wish you could find the right thing to say at the right moment. But we are not all blessed with a quick wit and those words never come when you most need them. You don't have to think of a fancy answer to a put down simply try these techniques.

Receiving Criticism

Nobody likes being criticized, particularly if it is unfair or constant. This may have been on your list of negative factors in Chapter One.

> **If someone is criticizing you it is imperative that first you get your inner voice right.**

Consider that the other person has a right to criticize you. If you do not do this then you will go on the defensive and behave aggressively. If you accept they have the right, then you will want them also to accept that you have the right not to be put down, or made to look small, or to be subjected to personal attacks. Also you have a right for that criticism to be made in private rather than in front of colleagues: 'Jane, can we discuss this in private please.'

If your inner voice is wrong for example: 'He's at it again, always nit picking. He's always got to find something wrong with what I do.' This will make you behave aggressively.

So listen to the voice inside your head, then challenge it and change into a positive inner voice.

> 'I have made a mistake but not necessarily a complete disaster.'

> 'The criticism may be a personal attack but I can get behind that and I can learn from it.'

If the criticism is unclear ask the other person for clarification. Use the 'I' statement assertively not aggressively: 'I'd find it helpful, Joe, if you could give me some examples of what you mean.' Again, we are using his name to help build rapport and make us sound more assertive.

If it becomes a personal attack: 'I accept that your criticism is valid, Laura, but I'd prefer it if you made it less of a personal attack.'

If you disagree with the criticism then say so. Use the I statement, 'As I see it...'

Maintain steady eye contact. Keep your voice clear and controlled. Don't get high pitched and indignant, 'You never told me *that*.'

If you are being subjected to constant criticism then ask yourself why? If you feel it is unjustified, or you are uncomfortable with it, then use the four part statement to tackle that person.

For example:

When you constantly criticize me Joe, **I feel** very annoyed **because** it is unjustified/becomes too much of a personal attack/is not specific enough. **I would appreciate** it if you made your criticism more specific by giving me examples of what you mean.'

Giving Criticism

Before giving criticism yourself check that your inner voice is sound and healthy. Also check that your criticism is specific and not a personal attack.

For example:

> 'James, I've noticed your reports have not been coming in on time. Can you tell me why this is?'

There is no excessive blaming here or jumping to conclusions.

In summary

O   Put downs can be extremely difficult to deal with

O   Put downs are designed to make you question your decisions and to belittle you

O   Put downs are a form of aggressive behaviour

O   When receiving criticism make sure your inner voice is right

O   Consider that the other person has a right to criticize you

O   You also have the right not to be put down, or made to look small, or be subjected to personal attacks

O   You have the right for criticism to be made in private

O   If the criticism is unclear ask the other person for clarification

O   If you disagree with the criticism then say so using the 'I' statement

- ○ Maintain steady eye contact. Keep your voice clear and controlled

- ○ Before giving criticism yourself check that your inner voice is positive

- ○ Check that your criticism is specific and not a personal attack

Chapter 13

Handling aggression and conflict

Conflict in your personal life and at work can arise for all sorts of reasons. It should be managed constructively to the benefit of everyone concerned.

Typical areas of conflict include:

○ mediating between two colleagues or two family members

○ a colleague who wants the same resources as you but thinks his need is greater

○ handling crises and unforeseen events

Handling Conflict

So how do you handle conflict? Do you become aggressive back? Do you give in at the expense of your own feelings? Do you handle it assertively? Or, as is

likely, do you resort to all three types of behaviour depending on what the conflict is and who is causing it?

First you need to understand your typical reactions to conflict. What do you usually do? Avoid them, confront them head on, or deal with them? Which things really annoy you and why? How do you feel at the time?

Exercise
Consider typical conflict situations, which you have encountered at work, at home, or in your social life. Write down what causes you conflict then write against it your typical reactions.

Now think whether or not this was the most appropriate response? What could have been the alternatives?

Does anything you've learned so far in this book help you? Could you have used the four part statement to deal with it? Could you have changed your inner voice to a more positive one and got a different result?

If someone is arguing with you do you immediately go on the defensive and argue back with your negative inner voice saying, 'How dare he talk to me like that?'

or 'How dare she think that her need is greater than mine?' How could you have changed this to a more positive inner voice?

When I meet anger, or hostility, instead of taking it as a personal attack I try and distance myself mentally from it by asking why the person is behaving in that manner. Sometimes there is no logical reason; perhaps this person continually irritates me because of a clash of personalities. If this is the case then my positive inner voice will say, 'I have difficulty in getting on with Jane, but I can keep calm and deal with her in a professional manner.' Or perhaps I can simply refuse to have anything to do with her, *if* I have the choice.

Think about the conflict situations where you generally avoid the issue. Is avoidance the best action for long-term benefit? Or does avoidance leave you feeling dejected or frustrated? If so what other alternatives are available?

I recall running a training course where one young lady was becoming particularly difficult, arguing with everything I was saying, not listening and trying to shout me and everyone else down. I heard my inner voice wishing she'd just shut up. I was getting angry inside

and then I was feeling resentful for even being there – in effect I was losing it.

Fortunately we were just on the lunch break so I called a halt to the session. I took the time out to get a positive inner dialogue, and then decided to confront the young lady.

I called her into a room to talk to her privately. I opened the conversation by saying that clearly she felt the course to be of no benefit to her and that if this were so she would be better off leaving; no one was forcing her to stay. I pointed out that there were others on the course who were enjoying it and found it beneficial, and that she was spoiling it for them. So, she had a choice, stay and benefit from the course, or leave? She chose to stay and, I am pleased to say, became a willing participant. Why? Because I had corrected my negative inner voice to a more positive one, which she responded to, and because I had confronted her about her behaviour instead of avoiding it.

Conflict often results from differences or perceived differences – try and understand the other person's viewpoint, and make sure you have a positive inner voice.

Blending with the other person can maximize similarities and minimize conflict. Use body language to enhance this, Mirror physical stance, match voice in volume and speed of conversation.

Exercise

Reflect on typical reactions to conflict situations and ask yourself:

O   When do I avoid conflict?

O   When do I accommodate others?

O   How often do I secure a compromise?

O   When do I compete strongly with others?

O   Which situations cause me to be bitter and resentful afterwards?

O   What alternatives are there for handling situations better?

If you get upset, try to remove yourself from the environment. Excuse yourself to go to the toilet or to return an urgent telephone call. Rehearse your four part statement if appropriate and/or get a positive inner voice; tell yourself you can deal with it. Calm yourself down before going back and resolving conflict.

And reward yourself every time you deal with a potentially awkward situation in a positive manner even if it is just giving yourself a pat on the back.

Handling aggression

Aggressive people can come at us out of the blue when we are least prepared for them. The attack can cause us to go into fight or flight mode i.e. to become aggressive or submissive. Ideally, however, we are seeking an assertive response to this attack that leaves us feeling neither cross or upset. The following way of dealing with aggression may help you. It is sometimes called the consequence method and it takes you through responses for handling escalating aggression.

Guidelines for handling aggression from others

Step 1

Take a breath and get a sound inner voice before you reply.

You will have time to do this as the angry person will be letting off a head of steam. Do not try to interrupt them when they are doing this, or try to reason with them, or you will only fuel their anger. You can never reason with people until they have worked their anger through. So whilst they are letting rip at you, take your breath and get your positive inner dialogue going. For example: 'I can handle this,' 'I can deal with this,' 'I can keep calm.' Tell yourself that this attack is not personal that something has happened to cause this person to behave like this and you happen to be the one they are taking it out on.

Step 2

Once they have calmed down you can then ask for clarification/information. Keep your tone of voice assertive and your eye contact steady. Keep your body posture upright. Ask open questions to get to the root cause of the problem: why, what, when, how, where, who.

Step 3

Hopefully by now the person will have calmed down, but what if they haven't? If the aggression is maintained then state where you stand but show you are interested in their opinion.

'I don't believe we have ignored your requests, Mr. Jones, but I'd like to hear why you think we have.'

Step 4

If the aggression is still maintained then step up your assertiveness. Increase the emphasis on your position.

'I believe I behaved appropriately.'

Step 5

If the aggression continues you can use the consequence. 'If you continue to shout in this way, Mr. Jones, I will put the phone down and ring you back later.'

Step 6

If all your efforts have failed either cut off the interaction – you have warned them – or put aside the issue you are discussing or arguing about and

try something like this, 'Look over the past three months we've spent lot of time arguing about this. Can we forget the procedure for the moment and talk about why we have these long arguments.'

I have only had to resort to using the consequence technique once in my career and that was when I was working in a busy inner city job centre. One of the clients starting shouting at me and being abusive. I warned him of the consequences if he continued to behave in that manner, and told him I would refuse to deal with him. He took no notice, so I carried out my threat. I had a great boss who backed me up and he told the man that until he could behave no one would deal with him.

It is a fact of life that you can't get on with everyone. You can't like everyone you work with, or come into contact with, but you may have to get along with them the best you can. If you can avoid them then do so; if not then don't waste your time, energy and emotions on becoming bitter and resentful. Life's too short for that. There are plenty of nice positive people out there. Give your difficult person a break and give yourself a break.

In summary

O   Conflict at home, in your personal life and at work can arise for all sorts of reasons

O   To handle conflict first understand what causes it

O   If a certain person causes you conflict then avoid him or her if you can

O   If you get upset, try to remove yourself from the environment

O   Rehearse your four part statement if appropriate and/or get a healthy inner voice, refresh yourself on your positive points and tell yourself you can deal with it

O   Calm yourself down before going back or resolving conflict

O   Reward yourself every time you deal with a potentially awkward situation in a positive manner even if it is just giving yourself a pat on the back

O   Aggressive situations hit us out of the blue when we are least prepared for them

O   The attack can cause us to go into fight or flight mode

O   Seek first to understand then to be understood

O   Think win -win versus win-lose

And Finally

Think positive to be a success

❑　Take 30 seconds each morning in front of a mirror.

❑　Just think what you want to happen during the day.

❑　Now verbalise this. Say it with conviction and with as much reassurance as you can muster. You may feel funny, you may laugh at this idea or yourself, but goad yourself on – go on be positive and see what happens.

❑　Go back to your personal objectives and goals. Believe you can do it.

❑　Visualize yourself achieving your personal goals.

❑　Affirm – say you can do it.

❑　Check that what you're going for is on target.

Take action.

Go for it.

Be positive and stay positive.

If you enjoyed this book and found it
helpful you may also enjoy:

Communicating with More Confidence

by Pauline Rowson

Communicating effectively should be the simplest
thing in the world, we talk and listen - or do we? And
is that all there is to it? When things go wrong in a
company, a friendship, a personal relationship,
communication or rather lack of it or misinterpreting
it, is often at the heart of the problem. Improving our
communication skills can bring huge rewards; it can
help us to win more contracts and sales, gain promotion,
find friendship, even love. It can enhance relationships
both at work and at home. This book provides tips and
techniques to improve communication skills and gain
the co-operation of others.

ISBN 09539856 9 5

www.rowmark.co.uk

Published by Rowmark Limited
65 Rogers Mead
Hayling Island
Hampshire
England
PO11 0PL

First published in 2002

Revised Edition 2007

ISBN 978-0-9548045-6-5

Printed by J. H. Haynes & Co. Ltd., Sparkford

The Easy Step by Step Guide to

BEING POSITIVE AND STAYING POSITIVE

(even when the going gets tough!)

PAULINE ROWSON

Revised Edition

ROWMARK